MAT YOGA FOR SENIORS WITH ARTHRITIS

Empowering Poses, Modifications and Mindfulness for Joint Health and Well-being

RANDY ROBERT

All rights reserved. No part of this publication may be reproduced, distributed, or transmitted in any form or by any means, including photocopying, recording, or other electronic or mechanical methods, without the prior written permission of the publisher, except in the case of brief quotations embodied in critical reviews and certain other noncommercial uses permitted by copyright law.

Copyright © Randy Robert, 2023.

TABLE OF CONTENT

INTRODUCTION

CHAPTER ONE

    1.1 Understanding Arthritis and Its Impact on Mobility

        1.2 Benefits of Yoga for Arthritis Management

        1.3 Precautions and Modifications for Arthritis Patients

        1.4 Creating a Safe and Supportive Yoga Practice

CHAPTER TWO

    Gentle Yoga Poses for Arthritis Relief

        2.1 Mindful Breathing and Relaxation Techniques for Pain Management

        2.2 Seated Yoga Poses for Joint Mobility and Flexibility

        2.3 Standing Yoga Poses for Balance and Strength

        2.4 Gentle Backbends and Twists for Spinal Health

CHAPTER THREE

Yoga Flows for Arthritis Management

        3.1 Slow Flow Sequences for Joint Warm-up and Increased Circulation

        3.2 Restorative Yoga Practices for Relaxation and Stress Reduction

CHAPTER FOUR

    Developing a Personalized Yoga Practice

        4.1 Designing a Yoga Routine for Arthritis

Symptoms and Individual Needs

4.2 Adapting Yoga Poses and Modifications for Different Types of Arthritis

4.3 Incorporating Props and Supports for Enhanced Comfort and Stability

4.4 Integrating Mindfulness and Meditation for Holistic Well-being

CONCLUSION

INTRODUCTION

With arthritis, millions of people throughout the world are affected by the condition. It is difficult to do the physical activities of daily living when there is inflammation, stiffness, and pain in the joints. The incorporation of gentle yoga into your daily routine, on the other hand, can provide numerous advantages for the management of arthritis.

Yoga can be broken down into its parts, which include mental and physical postures, breathing exercises, relaxation techniques, and mindfulness practices. It increases flexibility, balance, and strength in addition to strengthening the body, mind, and breath. Additional benefits include strengthening the body. By performing yoga, persons who suffer from arthritis can reduce the amount of pain they experience, improve their mobility, increase their strength, and enhance their mental health.

In this book, we will discuss the fundamentals of arthritis yoga and provide you with a variety of simple postures and sequences that are suitable for people who suffer from many different types of arthritis. During the practise, we will emphasize making changes, and alterations, and making use of props to guarantee that everyone is comfortable and safe. Regardless of your level of yoga ability, this book will guide you through a series of straightforward yoga poses and breathing exercises that can help alleviate the symptoms of arthritis.

Bear in mind at all times that your experience with arthritis will be unique in comparison to mine, and that the remedies that are effective for one person could not be effective for another. Before beginning a workout routine, it is important to pay attention to your body, be aware of your limits, and obtain either a medical clearance or the go-ahead from a licensed yoga instructor.

By adopting the peaceful movements of gentle yoga, you may be able to improve your quality of life, ease the symptoms of arthritic pain, and develop self-care. In preparation for this life-changing journey that we are about to embark on together, get ready to understand how gentle yoga can heal. Permit me to introduce you to the world of gentle yoga as a method for relieving the symptoms of arthritis.

CHAPTER ONE

1.1 Understanding Arthritis and Its Impact on Mobility

Arthritis is a long-term disorder that causes joint stiffness and inflammation. Hands, knees, hips, and spines are typical sites of manifestation, and it can impact individuals of any age. Different forms of arthritis, such as psoriatic arthritis, rheumatoid arthritis, and osteoarthritis, manifest in different ways and cause different kinds of pain.

Here we shall explore the various forms of arthritis and how they affect mobility in further detail. If you want your yoga practice to help alleviate the symptoms of arthritis, you need to know what those symptoms are. If you want to get the most out of your yoga practice while minimizing any pain associated with arthritis, it helps to have a better understanding of how the condition works.

Our focus will be on:

Joint cartilage degeneration causes osteoarthritis, the most prevalent kind of arthritis, which manifests as joint stiffness, discomfort, and limited mobility.

Joint deformities, exhaustion, and systemic symptoms are common outcomes of rheumatoid arthritis, an inflammatory disorder that causes persistent joint inflammation.

- Psoriatic Arthritis: Inflammation of the skin, joints, and lymph nodes; a form of arthritis that affects people with psoriasis.

- Effects on Mobility: Arthritis alters the range of motion, flexibility, and general physical function of affected joints. Arthritis is a prevalent condition, and we'll go over some of the difficulties people have and how yoga might help.

You can get the most out of gentle yoga if you take the time to learn about your arthritis and how it impacts your mobility. You will be able to safely and effectively alleviate your arthritis symptoms by incorporating this knowledge into your yoga practice and making informed decisions and adaptations along the way.

1.2 Benefits of Yoga for Arthritis Management

Arthritis sufferers can reap several emotional and physical benefits from yoga. Your general health can benefit from a yoga practice as part of your arthritis management plan. Here we'll take a look at some of the ways yoga can help those dealing with arthritis.

Advantages to Your Body:

1. Joint Mobility: The range of motion and flexibility of the joints can be enhanced via the practice of gentle yoga techniques. Stretching out the joints in a safe and

controlled manner is one of yoga's many benefits for mobility and joint stiffness.

The second benefit is increased stability and strength in the joints, which yoga poses provide by engaging and strengthening the muscles that surround the joints. By building strength in these areas, you can reduce strain on your joints and enhance their ability to move freely.

Thirdly, it improves balance, which in turn lowers the chance of damage from falls by increasing proprioception and stability via yoga's balancing postures. Confidence in performing everyday tasks can also be enhanced through improved balance.

4. Pain Relief: Yoga's relaxing practices, stretches, and light movements can be soothing for aching joints. One way that yoga can help alleviate the pain of arthritis is by stimulating the production of endorphins, which are the body's natural painkillers.

Fifth, work on your posture; a lot of people with arthritis have bad posture because their joints hurt and are stiff. Better posture and less joint strain are the results of yoga's ability to strengthen core muscles, enhance alignment, and correct imbalances.

Advantages for the Mind and Spirit:

First and foremost, yoga helps alleviate stress through its emphasis on deep breathing, meditation, and relaxation. Because stress can heighten arthritic symptoms and discomfort, stress management is crucial for those with this condition.

2. The Mind-Body Connection: Yoga promotes awareness and strengthens the bond between the two. A person's self-care and general health can benefit from this increased sensitivity to their body's signals.

3. Better Sleep: Yoga's calming and stress-relieving effects can help you get a better night's rest. A good night's sleep is

essential for recovery, immune system function, and general well-being.

4. Mental Health: Practising yoga daily can improve mental health, lessen anxiety, and boost mood. As well as fostering inner calm and satisfaction, yoga offers a constructive means of expressing one's individuality.

All of these advantages can be yours when you include yoga in your strategy for managing arthritis. Always go with your gut and do what makes you feel comfortable; remember that everyone's journey is unique. With consistent practice and proper instruction, yoga has the potential to alleviate arthritic symptoms and enhance overall well-being.

1.3 Precautions and Modifications for Arthritis Patients

The practice of yoga can help alleviate the symptoms of arthritis, but it's important to be careful and adjust as needed to avoid injury. Here we'll go over some extra safety measures and adjustments designed with arthritis sufferers in mind.

First and foremost, talk to your doctor before beginning any new workout routine. This is particularly true if you suffer from chronic pain, have any other health issues, or aren't sure if yoga would be a good fit for you.

2. Take It Easy at First: If you're new to yoga, it's best to ease into it with light, short sessions and build up to longer ones. Pay attention to your body and don't overdo it. To avoid overstressing your joints or getting hurt from a sudden acceleration, it's best to take it easy at first.

Third, Pay Attention to Both Pain and Discomfort: Although it's natural to feel some soreness or strain when stretching, you should never equate the two. Make adjustments or skip the posture if it hurts badly. Discover what works best for your body's range of motion.

4. Make Use of Props and Supports: When practicing yoga, it might be helpful to have a few extra items on hand, like blocks, bolsters, straps, and blankets, to help with stability and support. People with arthritis can adjust positions with their assistance, which reduces tension on the joints and makes them more accessible.

5. Adjust Pose Variations to Meet the Requirements of Arthritis. If you suffer from arthritis in your wrists, for instance, you can try doing yoga positions on your fists or using a wrist support. As an additional layer of protection, a folded blanket or pillow might alleviate the pain of arthritis in the knees.

6. Begin Your Yoga Practice with a Gentle Warm-Up and End with a Cool-Down. Some examples of this type of exercise are light stretching, range-of-motion drills, and joint mobilization. Likewise, make sure to incorporate a cooling-down phase into your

practice to help you relax and stretch out your muscles.

Breathe deeply and mindfully as you go through your practice; this brings us to our seventh point. In addition to calming the mind and body, this practice helps one tune into their breath and live in the here and now.

8. Pay Attention to Your Body: When you practice yoga, your body will show you the way. You should adjust or avoid a pose if it causes you pain or worsens your arthritis symptoms. Listen to your body and make changes when you feel the need.

Always keep in mind that you are not a cookie-cutter arthritis sufferer; what helps some may hurt others. Listen to your body and respect its limits; if you need help, find a yoga teacher who has experience teaching students with arthritis. You may make yoga a safe and helpful part of your arthritis care routine by following these guidelines and adjusting as needed.

1.4 Creating a Safe and Supportive Yoga Practice

People with arthritis must establish a yoga practice that is both safe and supportive. You may make sure that your yoga practice is both beneficial and fun by following some rules and taking some things into account. Here we will discuss some guidelines for developing a yoga practice that is both safe and supportive for those with arthritis.

1. Choosing an Appropriate Yoga Style: It is important to pick a yoga style that suits your requirements and capabilities. Because of its emphasis on relaxation and slow, controlled movements, gentle or restorative yoga is often appropriate for those with arthritis.

2. Locating an Experienced Teacher: If you suffer from arthritis, it's best to find a yoga teacher who has worked with patients who have this condition. To make sure your

practice is safe and effective, they can give you the right adjustments, point you in the right direction, and give you personalized support.

3. Warm-Up and Cool-Down: To get your muscles and joints ready for action and to improve blood circulation, start your practice with a light warm-up. Also, be sure to include a cool-down at the end of your practice so your body can relax and get back to its resting state.

4. Range of Motion and Gentle Movement: Prioritise light, fluid motions that increase flexibility and range of motion in the joints. To keep the joints from getting strained, refrain from aggressive or violent movements. Identify your pain threshold and work your way up to a more challenging range of motion.

5. Keep Your Balance: Make sure you're stable and in the correct position in every posture. To prevent injury to the joints,

engage the abdominal muscles and keep your body upright. Maintaining correct posture lessens strain on individual joints by distributing the body's weight more uniformly.

6. Make Use of Props and Supports: To make positions more accessible, use blocks, blankets, or straps as props to support your body. To improve safety and comfort, props can change postures, give support, and help keep the body in the correct alignment.

Seventh, Be Mindful: Make mindfulness a part of your yoga practice from the very beginning. Honor the here and now by paying close attention to your feelings, ideas, and bodily experiences. Recognizing your limitations, listening to your body, and making well-informed decisions are all benefits of practicing mindful awareness.

Be flexible and willing to change your poses regularly so that they work for you. Modify your poses to fit any restrictions or pain in your joints. Find out what modifications are available so that you can reap the advantages of a position without causing yourself any discomfort.

9. Recharge Your Batteries: Pay attention to when your body tells you it needs a break. Rest when you need to and don't push yourself too hard. In between yoga sessions, give your body a chance to heal and rejuvenate.

10. Take care of yourself and be compassionate with yourself when you do yoga. Never force yourself to do more than your body can handle, and remember to reward yourself for any and every improvement, no matter how tiny. The goal of yoga should not be perfection but rather the development of a healthy body and mind.

If you're an arthritis sufferer, you may make your yoga practice safe and beneficial by following these steps. Consistency, patience, and listening to your body are key. As you practice yoga regularly, you will feel better physically and mentally, and your arthritis symptoms will improve.

CHAPTER TWO

Gentle Yoga Poses for Arthritis Relief

2.1 Mindful Breathing and Relaxation Techniques for Pain Management

To alleviate pain, particularly chronic pain from diseases like arthritis, using relaxation techniques and mindful breathing might be helpful. You can relax more, feel less stressed, and have better health overall by doing these things. As a means of alleviating discomfort, this section will go over various relaxation and mindful breathing exercises.

Sit or lie down in a position that allows you to breathe deeply into your abdomen. Put your palms facing outward and your fingers crossed on your chest and belly. Bring your belly button up as you inhale slowly and deeply through your nose, taking a long, deep breath. As your belly button drops, gently let out a breath through your mouth. For a few minutes, just concentrate on your breathing and repeat this deep breathing rhythm. Relaxation and neural system calmness are both aided by deep abdominal breathing.

Step two: find a comfortable posture to sit or lie down and gradually relax your muscles. Lie down and focus on your body with your eyes closed. As you go down your body, progressively tighten and relax every muscle group, beginning with your toes. Breathe out any knots or sore spots in your body, paying attention to the feelings of tension and relaxation along the way. A feeling of general calm and relief from muscular tension can be yours with the help of progressive muscle relaxation.

Step Three: Collaborative Visualisation: Locate an Area of Serenity. Relax and let your mind wander to a peaceful location. A tranquil setting could be anything from a beach to a woodland. Get your senses working by filling your mind with the sights, sounds, smells, and textures of this made-up world. Put all of your worries and pains aside and allow yourself to be completely absorbed in this experience. One way to alleviate pain and induce calm is through a guided visualization.

The fourth step of body scan meditation is to find a relaxed position, like a chair or a bed. Lie down and focus on your body with your eyes closed. Scan your entire body, paying close attention to each section, starting at the crown of your head. Keep an eye out for any pain, tightness, or other unpleasant feelings. Feel the stress melt away and welcome tranquility as you focus on every part of your body. One way to relax and connect with your body is to do a body scan meditation.

As a fifth form of meditation, mindfulness encourages you to sit comfortably and focus on the here and now. Keep your attention on your breath, allowing yourself to just notice each inhalation and exhale. Recognize any feelings or ideas that pop into your head and then gently redirect your focus to your breathing if you need to. Try this out for a while—a few minutes or more, it's up to you. Through the practice of nonjudgmental awareness, which is a hallmark of mindfulness meditation, one can learn to relax and unwind more easily.

To properly manage pain, incorporate these breathing and relaxation techniques into your everyday practice. Always keep in mind that your experience with pain and relaxation techniques may differ from someone else's; so, it is crucial to discover the methods that help you the most. Better health, less discomfort, and more relaxation are all possible outcomes of regular practice and patience.

2.2 Seated Yoga Poses for Joint Mobility and Flexibility

If you suffer from arthritis or have trouble with weight-bearing exercises, sitting yoga postures may help increase your flexibility and range of motion in your joints. For these positions, you can use a chair or props to help you get into a floor position. To strengthen various joints, try these sitting yoga poses:

A seated neck stretch entails sitting up straight in a chair or lying on one's back with one's feet flat on the floor. Try bringing your right ear closer to your right shoulder while simultaneously stretching your left side of the neck. Maintain for a few breaths before alternating sides. To alleviate stiffness and tightness in the neck, stretch it out a few times on each side.

2. Seated Spinal Twist: Lie on your back with your legs extended and one foot flat on the floor. Rest your right hand on top of

your left thigh. With a long, deep breath in, straighten your spine. Then, with a quick twist of your torso to the left, gaze over your left shoulder. Remain gently stretched while holding the twist for several breaths. Do the same thing over on the opposite side. Relaxation and increased spinal mobility are two benefits of this posture.

Seat with your legs spread wide in front of you for the third posture, the seated forward fold. Breathe in deeply and let your spine extend. As you breathe out, bring your hands to your feet in a forward hinge. If it helps, you can wrap a towel or strap around your feet to make the forward fold easier. Avoid bending over or hunching over by maintaining a straight spine. You may increase your hip flexibility, stretch your lower back, and loosen your hamstrings by striking this pose.

The fourth position is the seated ankle-to-knee pose, which entails sitting up straight in a chair or lying on the floor.

Cross your right ankle over your left knee and let your right knee lean to one side. Bend over to shield your knee. Keep your body in this position if you experience any hip stretches. To achieve a more profound stretch, gently bend forward from the hips while maintaining a straight back. Do the same thing over on the opposite side. Flexing your hip flexors and glutes in this position might help you move about more freely.

Fifth, the seated butterfly pose: sit tall on the floor or a chair and bring your foot soles together, letting your knees hang loosely to the sides. Keep your grip on your foot or ankles and bend at the knees slightly so they touch the floor. As you loosen and open your hips, take a few deep breaths. Increase your range of motion in your hips and inner thighs with this posture.

When practicing these seated yoga positions, keep in mind that your body has limitations that must be respected. Make adjustments to the postures or consult a trained yoga professional if you feel any pain or restriction. When practiced regularly, these seated positions can enhance flexibility, mobility, and general health.

2.3 Standing Yoga Poses for Balance and Strength

When you do standing yoga poses, you will increase your stability, strength, and balance. In addition to increasing self-awareness, they work a variety of muscle areas. A few standing yoga postures that are known to increase strength and stability are:

The first position, known as Mountain Pose (Tadasana), is to stand with your legs wide apart and your toes pointed forward. Even out your weight distribution between your two feet. Lift your kneecaps, extend your spine, and tense your leg muscles. Take a moment to relax your shoulders and raise your arms parallel to the floor. To help you center and steady yourself, hold this position for a few breaths.

To enter the Tree Pose (Vrikshasana), place your right foot under your left. Lay your right foot on top of your left inner thigh, toes pointing down. Alternatively, you can rest your right foot on your left ankle or calf if maintaining your balance becomes difficult. Lower your palms towards your navel or raise them towards the sky. You can find some balance by focusing on one thing. Stay in the position for a few breaths before switching sides. You can strengthen your legs, focus better, and increase your balance by doing tree posture.

Step three, Warrior II (Virabhadrasana II): Stand with your feet wide apart, leading with your right foot and slightly inward-turned left foot. Stand with your left leg straight and your right knee bent, keeping it above your ankle. With your palms facing outward, parallel to the floor, look over your right index finger. Pump your glutes and feel the power in your lower body. Maintain the position for a few breaths before switching sides. Improve your balance, hip mobility, and leg strength with Warrior II.

4. First, stand with your feet hip-width apart. This is the Chair Pose or Utkatasana. Praying with palms facing each other, exhale, and bring your arms up to your chest. Let go of your breath and lower your knees, as if settling back into a made-up chair. Bend at the waist and stretch your spine while you stand on your heels. Breathe into the position and hold it for a few breaths to feel your abs and legs strengthen. Stability and leg strength are both enhanced in the chair stance.

Fifth, stand with your feet hip-width apart in Warrior I (Virabhadrasana I). Step back three or four steps while turning your left foot slightly inward. While maintaining a straight line from your right knee to your ankle, bend it. Your left heel should be firmly planted on the ground. Praying with palms facing each other, exhale, and bring your arms up to your chest. Raise your arms upward and bring your hips and shoulders into a square. Maintain the position for a few breaths before switching sides. Improving balance, opening the chest, and strengthening the legs are all goals of Warrior I.

Pay attention to how you feel and only do what you can do when exercising. These standing poses can be practiced with the help of a chair or wall if necessary. When you start to feel stronger and more balanced, you should gradually ramp up the time and effort you put into your practice. Standing yoga positions like these can help you feel more grounded and present, strengthen your muscles, and increase your overall stability.

2.4 Gentle Backbends and Twists for Spinal Health

When practiced regularly, light twists and backbends can help alleviate back pain, increase flexibility, and keep the spine in good health. The spinal muscles are stretched and strengthened in these positions, which also improves mobility and range of motion. Soft twists and backbends like these can be a part of your practice:

1. Sphinx Pose: Lie on your stomach and bring your elbows under your shoulders. Bring your forearms down parallel to the ground. Stand with your lower body relaxed and your forearms pressed against the ground. Lift your chest gently. Look ahead while you straighten your back, tuck your shoulders in, and lift your hips. Count to ten while you hold the position, allowing your front body and spine to gently expand.

2. The Cat-Cow Pose: Upon descending onto your hands and knees, locate your wrists

beneath your shoulders and place your knees beneath your hips. Take a tabletop position. Cow Pose is an inhalation-based yoga posture that involves raising the tailbone, arching the back, and pulling the chest forward. The Cat Pose entails pulling your chin in towards your chest, rounding your spine, and tucking your tailbone as you exhale. While breathing in and out of each position, you may warm up and mobilize your spine in a steady progression.

3. The Supported Bridge Pose, which entails lying on one's back with one leg bent and one foot flat on the floor, hip-width apart. Lay down on a yoga block or a folded blanket beneath your sacrum, which is the bony area at the base of your spine. To make a slight bend in your back, press your feet down and elevate your hips. Put your weight on the prop and relax your glutes. Consider the relief in your lower back and the opening in your front as you remain in the pose for a few breaths.

4. Seated Spinal Twist — Lie on your back and extend your legs out in front of you. Step one: squat down with your right leg bent and left foot flat on the floor. Before you twist your torso to the right, stretch your spine and inhale. With your left hand on the outside of your right leg and your right hand behind you for support, rotate your torso, and exhale. Be careful to maintain a long spine as you gently deepen the twist with each exhalation. Do the same thing over on the opposite side. When you sit in a twisting motion, you can reduce back pain and increase spinal mobility.

5. The Poised Child: Set yourself up on your heels and knees. Maintain contact between your big toes and spread your knees wide. Stretch your spine as you take a deep breath in. With an exhale, bring your hands to the right side of your body, letting your torso twist and rest on your right thigh. Under your torso, you can lay a folded blanket or bolster for support. Feel the strain in your spine as you breathe deeply into the twist.

Do the same thing over on the opposite side. A great way to unwind and relieve stress, this position twists and stretches the spine softly.

Pay attention to your breath and your body as you progress into each pose; you want to avoid strain and suffering by moving gently and deliberately. To avoid aggravating any existing back problems, it's best to seek the advice of a doctor or certified yoga teacher before attempting these positions. A healthy spine, more flexibility, and a relaxed back are all benefits of a regular practice of light twists and backbends.

CHAPTER THREE

Yoga Flows for Arthritis Management

3.1 Slow Flow Sequences for Joint Warm-up and Increased Circulation

A slow flow sequence is a great way to loosen up those joints, get your blood pumping, and reawaken your body. The fluid motions in these sequences are timed to the breath. In addition to fostering a feeling of stability and calm, they aid in increasing range of motion and flexibility. Consider this example of a sluggish flow sequence:

1. Stand with your feet hip-width apart in a forward fold (Uttanasana). As you take a deep breath in, raise your arms above your head. Then, as you let your breath out, bend forward from your hips and let your head

and neck relax. To alleviate strain on the lower back, bend at the knees if necessary. For a deeper stretch, hold onto opposite elbows and sway gently from side to side, letting gravity do the work. While holding this position, take a few deep breaths and focus on the sensations of releasing tension in your legs and stretching your spine.

2. Urdhva Hastasana, or Extended Mountain Pose: Breathe deeply and slowly raise your arms aloft. Put your hands facing up and interlace your fingers. Look up and slightly bend your back, arching your upper back. Make sure your legs are fully extended and your feet firmly planted on the ground. As you open your shoulders and let your muscles relax in the front of your body, take a few long breaths.

3. Strike a cat-cow pose by bringing your knees to rest on a tabletop and placing your hands beneath your shoulders. Take a deep breath in, lower your tummy, and then elevate your head and tailbone into Cow

Pose. To enter Cat Pose, breathe out and roll your shoulders back while tucking your chin and tailbone. Move slowly and deliberately between the two positions as you breathe in and out. Pay attention to how your spine moves and how your back gently stretches.

4. Step forward with your right foot interlocked with your hands, and bring your left knee down to the floor in a low lunge (Anjaneyasana). Remember to keep your right knee bent over your ankle. Straighten your back and put your palms on your right thigh. Lift your arms aloft while maintaining a relaxed posture if you find it comfortable. Hold the position for a few breaths, allowing yourself to feel the hip flexor stretch and the mild opening of the chest.

5. Adho Mukha Svanasana, or Downward Facing Dog, requires you to come forward from a low lunge, meeting your right foot at the top of the mat. Bend over at the waist and put your palms flat on the floor, shoulder-width apart. Form an inverted

V-shape by walking your hands forward while lifting your hips. Maintain a relaxed neck position while pressing your palms to the floor and engaging your abs. The hamstrings and calves can be stretched by pedaling your feet. Feel the freedom in your shoulders and the stretch in your back legs as you take many deep breaths in this position.

6. Bring your knees to the ground and sit back on your heels in Child's Pose (Balasana), which is a variation of Downward Facing Dog. Bring your arms forward and fold your chest forward so that your forehead touches the mat. Allow your whole body to sink into the pose as you loosen your shoulders. Relax and center yourself by taking a few long, deep breaths and letting them flow through your body.

Focus on your breath and the sensations throughout your body as you repeat this slow flow sequence several times. Do what works best for your body and joints, and don't be afraid to experiment with different versions. Whether you're doing yoga or just want to start your day off well, this sequence will help you feel more limber and more energized.

3.2 Restorative Yoga Practices for Relaxation and Stress Reduction

If you're looking for a way to unwind and calm down, try some restorative yoga. They let the body and mind relax deeply via the practice of holding gentle, supported positions for extended times. Some gentle yoga poses that can help you relax and recharge are:

1. Kneel with your legs spread wide and your big toes touching in the Supported Child's Pose. On top of your mat, put a bolster or folded blankets. In this forward fold, with your head turned to one side, put your torso on the bolster or blankets. Let your arms loosen up with the props. Holding this position for a few minutes will help you

release stress and tension in your body while you breathe deeply and slowly.

2. The Legs-Up-The-Wall Pose (Viparita Karani): Lie on your back with your legs resting on a wall. Sit on one side next to a wall. Find a comfortable position where your sitting bones are parallel to the wall. Keep your arms at your sides and turn your palms upward. Relax your whole body by closing your eyes. When you strike this posture, you can ease nervous system tension, weariness, and anxiety.

3. Supta Baddha Konasana, or Supported Reclining Bound Angle Pose: On your mat, lay a bolster or two folded blankets lengthwise. Sit in a bent kneeling position with your foot soles touching; let your knees hang loosely to the sides. Put the bolster in a position that will allow it to support your full spine when you lie back. Keep your palms facing up and your arms relaxed at your sides. Put your gaze down and let the supports carry you as you give in to the

position. In addition to encouraging profound relaxation, this posture aids in opening the chest, hips, and inner thighs.

4. For Supported Savasana, choose a cozy spot and prop up your body with pillows, bolsters, or blankets. To support your lower back's natural curvature while you lie on your back, put a bolster or folded blankets under your knees. If you need more support for your head and neck, use a folded blanket underneath. Lay flat on your back with your arms and legs extended, palms facing up. Put all of your attention on your breathing while you close your eyes and let your body relax. Hold this position for ten to fifteen minutes, or until you feel completely relaxed and able to release any stress or tension.

5. Front-Supported Fold: Take a seat on a bolster or a pile of folded blankets. Lay your upper body on the bolster or blankets as you fold forward, legs spread wide in front of you. Hold your head up using your hands or other objects as necessary. Relax into the

pose and breathe deeply and slowly as you let go of all resistance. To alleviate stress and anxiety, try this posture. It will help you relax your back, shoulders, and neck.

You should keep in mind that the main goal of restorative yoga is to help you relax and feel comfortable. Make the poses seem easy by using props to support your body. Give yourself enough time to fully relax into each pose by staying in them for long periods. If you want to get into the zone as you practice, find a dark, peaceful place and maybe even put on some gentle music.

3.3 Yoga Nidra for Deep Relaxation and Restorative Sleep

Yoga Nidra is an effective method for rejuvenating sleep and profound relaxation. As you follow the instructions of a trained meditation instructor, your muscles and mind will gradually relax, allowing you to enter a deep level of relaxation and renewal.

A detailed instruction on how to do Yoga Nidra is as follows:

1. Get Ready for practice by Locating a Convenient Spot to Lie Down on Your Back. Get yourself a yoga mat or find a plush carpet to work on. Throw a blanket over you to be warm and cozy. To provide even more support, you can place a pillow or bolster beneath your knees.

2. Make a Goal: Before you begin your practice, sit down and make a goal for yourself. Wanting to unwind, sleep well, or relieve stress and tension are all examples of basic needs. While you practice, keep this goal in your mind and visualize it.

3. Progressive Relaxation: Starting on the right side of your body, bring your focus to different sections of your body. Gently and methodically move your focus from one portion of your body to another, allowing yourself to relax as you go. Beginning with your right hand, you can progress to your

right arm, shoulder, and, finally, the right side of the chest. Do the same thing with your left side.

Fourth, become aware of your breath by directing your attention there. Without attempting to alter it, simply watch the natural cadence of your breath. Pay close attention to the feeling of your breath coming in and going out. If you're already feeling relaxed, this will help you relax even more.

5. Create a positive affirmation, also known as a Sankalpa, in your thoughts. A brief, encouraging comment that is in line with your goal will do. With full conviction and belief, repeat this affirmation three times silently to yourself.

6th, Visualisation: Following the instructions of the Yoga Nidra practice, start to picture various scenes or events. Following the directions will take you on a visual journey through a variety of settings, such as a serene forest, a beach, or a condition of pure pleasure. Just do as it says and let your mind wander freely through the visualizations.

7. Body Sensations: Direct your focus to more nuanced feelings throughout your body. Pay attention to different feelings, such as heat, weight, lightness, or tingling, as the instructions lead you to do so. Pay attention to these feelings without attaching any significance to them.

A gentle return to the here and now will be offered by the guide as you near the finish of the Yoga Nidra practice, which is the eighth and final step. Breathe deeply, wiggle your toes and fingers, and gradually reintroduce movement to your body. Do not rush the process of returning to a seated position.

While there is no set time limit for practicing Yoga Nidra, even a brief session of fifteen to twenty minutes can have a profoundly restorative effect. It works wonders for enhancing general health, facilitating profound relaxation, decreasing tension, and enhancing the quality of sleep. You might want to think about downloading an app or listening to a guided Yoga Nidra audio to help you practice.

CHAPTER FOUR

Developing a Personalized Yoga Practice

4.1 Designing a Yoga Routine for Arthritis Symptoms and Individual Needs

A yoga program that is individualized for the treatment of arthritic symptoms should be built on the foundation of mindful movements, joint mobilization, and gentle movements. The following is an example of a yoga routine that could be used to treat arthritic pain:

Before beginning an exercise program, it is essential to consult with a physician or a physical therapist. These professionals can evaluate your health and provide guidance that is tailored to your specific requirements and condition. Therefore, it is essential to seek their opinion before beginning an exercise program.

A light warm-up should be performed at the beginning of your routine to get your blood pumping and your muscles ready to move. Rolling the shoulders, making circles with the wrists, and rotating the ankles are all examples of gentle motions that can be incorporated into this. Additional examples include rolling the shoulders.

When it comes to mobility, it is important to pay attention to light motions that can improve the health of the joints and increase mobility. By performing range-of-motion exercises such as knee bends, ankle pumps, shoulder circles, and wrist circles, one can achieve joint lubrication and a reduction in stiffness. Move forward with caution, keeping a close eye out for any pain or discomfort that may occur.

4. Lightweight Asanas: When practicing yoga, it is important to go for positions that

are both flexible and strong, but do not put an excessive amount of strain on the joints. The following are some examples of asanas that may be beneficial for people who suffer from arthritis:

To achieve Tadasana, also known as Mountain Pose, you must stand tall with your feet hip-width apart and your ankles fully extended. As you straighten your back and relax your shoulders, take a few deep breaths in and bring them to your chest.

Your spine will gently arch and round as you transition between the two positions of the Cat-Cow Pose (Marjaryasana-Bitilasana). This will happen as you breathe in and out of the pose. This has several benefits, two of which are the reduction of strain on the back and the enhancement of mobility in the spine.

4.2 Adapting Yoga Poses and Modifications for Different Types of Arthritis

Supported Bridge Pose, also referred to as Setu Bandha Sarvangasana, is a yoga position in which you lie on your back. Your knees should be bent, and your feet should be spread hip-distance apart. A block or bolster should be placed under your sacrum to provide support for your lower back and hips. As you relax into this yoga position, your chest will open up, and your hip flexors will be stretched.

In the case that you require assistance with Supported Tree Pose (Vrksasana), you can either stand next to a wall or make use of a chair to assist you. Position your foot so that it is on the inside of the other leg, either the thigh or the calf, to find your equilibrium. Avoid putting any weight on the joint that is injured. By striking this pose, you can improve your balance and strengthen your legs at the same time.

- The Seated Forward Fold, also known as Paschimottanasana, is a yoga position in which the practitioner sits on the edge of a folded blanket with their legs spread wide apart. Bend forward at the hips and reach for your feet after you have accomplished the task of lengthening your spine. Wrapping a towel around your feet or using a strap are two options to consider if you are having difficulty getting to your feet. This pose allows you to stretch your back, hamstrings, and calves into a more relaxed state.

The Modified Child's Pose, also known as Balasana, is achieved by increasing the width of your knees and bringing your big toes together. This pose begins with you kneeling. Sitting back on your heels and folding forward while placing a blanket or bolster under your forehead is the way to practice this technique. While you are in this position, your lower back, hips, and thighs will be lightly stretched, which will help you relax.

You can improve your ability to relax and deal with stress by incorporating meditation and deep breathing into your daily routine. This will help you unwind and manage stress more effectively. Through the practice of mindfulness meditation and deep belly breathing exercises, one can improve their ability to manage pain, stress, and their overall mental and physical health.

6. De-stress and Cool Down: At the end of your practice, you should perform a light de-stress that includes slow, deliberate movements and relaxation positions. The final pose of yoga practice, Savasana, also referred to as corpse pose, is an excellent way to wind down because it allows both your body and mind to relax into the pose and take in all of the benefits that it offers.

At all times, pay attention to your body and make adjustments or avoid movements or positions that cause you discomfort. Continue to focus on what you are good at, and make adjustments as you go along. The practice of yoga for arthritis requires consistent practice, patience, and an approach that is slow and steady.

When adapting yoga poses to accommodate different types of arthritis, the guiding principles that should be followed are to put the patient's comfort, joint protection, and pain management at the forefront. The following are some general suggestions for modifying yoga poses that are intended for individuals who suffer from common forms of arthritis:

It is most common for osteoarthritis to manifest itself in the joints that are subjected to the greatest amount of pressure from our body's weight, such as the knees, hips, and spine. During the process of planning postures to alleviate osteoarthritis—

It is recommended that you make use of bolsters, blankets, or blocks as props to maintain the correct position and support of your joints. During yoga poses, you might find it helpful to sit on a chair or a block to reduce the amount of pressure that is placed on your knees.

- Reduce your mobility as much as possible: If you find that you have too much mobility, adjust your poses so that you have less mobility. For instance, rather than folding deeply into a forward fold, you should keep a slight bend in your knees throughout the exercise.

Stay away from positions that put an excessive amount of strain on the joints that are affected. By avoiding forward bends and other positions that put an excessive amount of pressure on the joints of the wrists and hands, individuals who suffer from arthritis in those areas should do their best to avoid these positions.

This autoimmune disorder, known as rheumatoid arthritis, is characterized by the destruction of the small joints throughout the body, most notably those found in the hands, feet, and wrists. When adjusting yoga positions for people with rheumatoid arthritis:

Work on mild motions that increase the range of motion in the joints without inflaming them. This is an important part of the exercise routine. When compared to activities that are quick or repetitive, movements that are slow and controlled typically produce better results.

Use straps, blocks, or blankets as support items when necessary; they can be helpful in a variety of situations. As a consequence of this, you might experience less discomfort and less strain on your joints.

- If you are experiencing discomfort from weight-bearing poses, you should try modifying them. Take, for instance, the modified plank pose; rather than using your hands, you should try exercising with your forearms.

It is important to be aware of the limitations of your joints and to avoid overextending yourself; doing so will assist you in remaining within your comfort zone. If your body is telling you to do so, make adjustments or skip poses as the situation warrants.

Psoriatic arthritis is the third type of arthritis, and it can affect both the skin and the joints. Its severity can range from mild discomfort to severe pain. When making adjustments to poses, psoriatic arthritis patients should:

Variations that are easy on the joints: When selecting variations of poses, it is important to select variations that are easy on the joints. This will allow you to support yourself and prevent strain. In place of high lunges, you can perform low lunges, which involve placing the back knee on the floor in a stationary position.

With the help of additional padding, such as blankets or towels, you can prevent areas of your body that have sensitive skin or plaques caused by psoriasis from coming into contact with the floor or props while you are performing poses that require supporting the skin.

Joints that are painful or inflamed should not be subjected to unnecessary pressure, and you should exercise caution when moving them. Pay attention to any soreness or inflammation that you experience. To avoid making the inflammation worse, it is important to avoid overstretching or twisting the area too deeply. Instead, you should focus on movements that are slow and light.

You must seek the advice of a yoga instructor or therapist who is trained in the practice if you suffer from arthritis or any other joint condition. You can fine-tune your practice with their assistance because they can tailor their recommendations, suggestions, and modifications to align with your specific needs. Under no circumstances should you start an exercise program without first consulting with a healthcare professional, paying attention to your body, and working out within your fitness level of comfort.

4.3 Incorporating Props and Supports for Enhanced Comfort and Stability

If you are afflicted with arthritis or any other form of joint condition, you might discover that incorporating props and supports into your yoga practice can significantly enhance both your level of comfort and stability. The following is a list of common props and the application of each:

1. Yoga blocks: These versatile props can be used for a variety of purposes, including modifying poses and providing support. They can also be used to modify poses. By bringing the floor closer to you, you will find

it much simpler to strike poses. You can use them to accomplish this. Take this example as an example:

When you are performing the standing forward fold, you might want to try placing blocks under your hands to alleviate pressure on your lower back and hamstrings.

When practicing seated poses, sitting on a block can help alleviate muscle pain in the hips and knees.

2. Which is an excellent material for providing both support and comfort. They can provide stability and alleviate pain in a variety of positions for the user. For example, the following are some kneeling poses, such as the Hero's Pose (Virasana): It is possible to use a folded blanket as a cushion or support under the hips or knees.

It is recommended that you make use of a blanket to support your head and neck while you are lying down in a position such as Savasana (Corpse Pose).

3. Bolsters: These cushions are large and firm, and their purpose is to provide support and ensure that you remain in the correct position. The use of these poses for relaxation and restorative purposes can be quite beneficial. For example, if you are experiencing lower back pain and want to encourage relaxation while practicing Savasana, you should place a bolster under your knees.

Supported Bridge Pose is a straightforward backbend that calls for the utilization of a bolster to lengthen the spine.

4. Yoga straps: These help maintain your body in the correct alignment, extending into deeper poses, and increasing your physical flexibility. They have the potential to save lives in situations where movement in the joints is restricted. Take this example as an example:

Using a strap can significantly increase your range of motion, which is beneficial for exercises such as seated forward folds and hamstring stretches. By wrapping a strap around the foot, you can assist in elevating the legs while performing supine leg stretches.

When you are in a standing or balance pose, you can lean on a wall or a chair for additional support. This is in addition to the fact that you can lean on a chair. In the case of standing poses such as the Half Moon Pose or the Tree Pose, for example: - Make use of a chair as a device.

You should lean on a wall for support whenever you are standing or performing a modified version of the Downward Dog.

The purpose of props and supports is to assist you in achieving poses that are more physically accessible, comfortable, and secure. Through experimentation with the props and making adjustments to them as required, you can determine the amount of support that your body requires. If you are unsure of what to do or what kinds of props to use, a certified yoga instructor can demonstrate to you how to properly use props and make recommendations regarding which ones will be most beneficial to your practice.

4.4 Integrating Mindfulness and Meditation for Holistic Well-being

By incorporating meditation and mindfulness into your yoga practice, you can significantly improve not only your physical health but also your mental and emotional well-being. The following is a list of some of the ways that you can incorporate mindfulness and meditation into your daily routine:

1. Mindful Awareness: During every yoga session, make it a point to remain one hundred percent present. Pay attention to the sensations in your body, the quality of

your breathing, and any thoughts or feelings that come to the surface. This will help you concentrate on the here and now. Maintain an emotionless and judgment-free focus on the events that are taking place right now.

2. Practise mindfulness of the breath by focusing your attention on the rhythm of your breath to bring you back to the present moment. Keep a record of your breathing pattern and center yourself around it as you work on your breathing technique. Pay close attention to each breath as it enters and exits your body; if your thoughts wander, gently bring them back to the breath. Maintain this awareness throughout the entire process.

3. Either before or after your yoga session, you should try something called a body scan meditation. Your awareness should be brought to each area of your body as you move down your body, beginning at the top of your head and ending at your toes. As you do so, you should take note of any feelings,

whether they be tightness or relaxation. You should make an effort to relax and accept each part of your body as you move through it.

Practicing mindful movement, also known as entering each yoga pose with an open mind and a specific intention, is the fourth principle. As you transition from one asana (posture) to the next, rather than trying to force yourself into the next one, you should concentrate on the sensations in your body, the alignment, and your breath. Always remember to keep your attention on the here and now as well as the sensation of each movement.

Loving-kindness meditation practice should be performed for a few minutes before you wind down your practice, as the fifth step. Feel free to send love and kindness to yourself, your loved ones, and everything else that is alive. If you want to get into the habit of saying positive affirmations, you should try repeating phrases like "May I be happy, may I be healthy, and may I live with ease" over and over again.

Mindfulness with Savasana (Corpse Pose): During this time, you should take the opportunity to meditate and relax deeply. While you allow your body to sink into the floor, relax your muscles and concentrate on your breathing or anything else you choose to do throughout this time. Allow yourself to be present in the here and now, letting go of your worries and thoughts.

Incorporate Mindfulness and Meditation Into Your Everyday Life Take your mindfulness and meditation practices outside of the realm of yoga and incorporate them into your day-to-day life. While you are eating, walking, or engaging in any of your other routine activities, make sure that you are fully present and aware. Always remember to take a break from whatever it is that you are doing so that you can concentrate on the here and now.

Remember that the skills of meditation and mindfulness require consistent practice. This is something you should always keep in mind. Begin with shorter bursts to get a sense of the duration, and then gradually increase the length of your workouts. You should approach these practices with an attitude of openness and curiosity, and you should also treat yourself with patience. Your regular yoga practice has the potential to assist you in achieving greater health and tranquility if you regularly engage in it.

CONCLUSION

This book has discussed a variety of topics, including how to incorporate mindfulness and meditation into yoga for overall health, as well as how to modify poses to accommodate different types of arthritis. The guidelines and suggestions have proven to be of great assistance to individuals who are concerned about the possibility of practicing yoga while also dealing with arthritis.

An overarching theme that can be found throughout the book is the modification of yoga poses to meet particular requirements, the reduction of pain, and the protection of joints. By utilizing props and modifications, individuals who suffer from arthritis can make yoga more accessible, stable, and comfortable for themselves. Finding a professional yoga instructor or therapist is essential if you want to receive individualized attention and support while you are practicing yoga.

In addition to the importance of mindfulness and meditation, which we have already covered, the promotion of overall health is also an important factor. Meditation on the breath, body scans, and mindful movement are all examples of mindfulness practices that can assist an individual in becoming more attuned to the sensations that occur within their body, more fully present in the here and now, and more accepting of themselves and the limitations that they possess. It is possible to bring the benefits of mindfulness out of the yoga mat and into your everyday life by incorporating loving-kindness meditation and mindful living into your daily routine.

It is important to keep in mind that the experience of living with arthritis is unique for each individual, and adjustments should be made following the specific requirements and limitations of each individual. Consult your physician before beginning a new fitness or wellness program, especially if you have any preexisting conditions. This is especially important if you have any health conditions.

By modifying yoga poses, making use of props, and incorporating mindfulness and meditation into their practice, individuals who suffer from arthritis can find relief from the physical, mental, and emotional symptoms that they experience. It is possible to alleviate the symptoms of arthritis, improve joint health, and foster overall wellness by regularly practicing yoga and carrying out the practice with an attitude of patience, self-compassion, and dedication.

With the specific requirements and capabilities of people who live with arthritis in mind, I hope that this book will serve as a useful resource and a guide for you as you embark on a journey toward a yoga practice that leaves you feeling more fulfilled and enriched. As you practice with compassion, mindfulness, and a strong connection to your body, I hope that your life is filled with harmony and that your health improves.

Printed in Great Britain
by Amazon